Crimson Sunshine

Reflections with Poetry & Prose

JESSICA WEYER BENTLEY

ARTWORK BY
LAURA BENTLEY

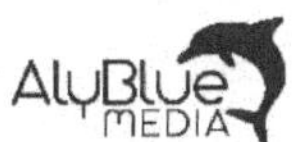

Crimson Sunshine
Reflections with Poetry & Prose – 1st ed.
Jessica Weyer Bentley
Artwork by Laura Bentley

Cover Design by AlyBlue Media, LLC
Interior Design by AlyBlue Media LLC
Published by AlyBlue Media, LLC
AlyBlue Media www.AlyBlueMedia.com

ISBN: 978-1-944328-94-8
AlyBlue Media, LLC
Ferndale, WA 98248
www.AlyBlueMedia.com

This book is designed to provide informative narrations to readers. It is sold with the understanding that the writers, authors or publisher is not engaged to render any type of psychological, legal, or any other kind of professional advice. The content is the sole expression and opinion of the authors and writers. No warranties or guarantees are expressed or implied by the choice to include any of the content in this book. Neither the publisher nor the author or writers shall be liable for any physical, psychological, emotional, financial, or commercial damages including but not limited to special, incidental, consequential or other damages.

PRINTED IN THE UNITED STATES OF AMERICA

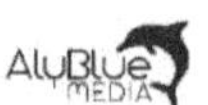

CRIMSON SUNSHINE

Dedication

For Peg—
You took a chance on me, taught me
love, and gave me a loving and solid
foundation to follow my dreams.

Contents

BY BRIAN R. HALL

Foreword

It is an honor and privilege to write the foreword for *Crimson Sunshine*. Having gone to school with Jessica Weyer Bentley in the mountains of eastern Kentucky, we share a common bond of an Appalachian cultural upbringing. I later found we had another commonality—a passion for writing.

I was filled with excitement when Jessica first told me she was penning a book. We immediately began discussing books and writing projects, sharing experiences with all the ins and outs of writing and creating.

The Appalachian Mountains of eastern Kentucky have produced some of the best musicians, artists, craftsmen, and entertainers in the world. Few would guess that such a rural, sparsely populated area isolated by forests and mountains could produce such a quantity of quality creative talent. With all honesty, Jessica has shown herself to be a shining part, and will soon become a widely recognized icon of the Appalachian celebrity talent scene.

When I received a prerelease copy of *Crimson Sunshine*, I told myself I would start by reading just a few pages to get a feel for the book and Jessica's writing style. I had been very busy working on four books and two film scripts, so planned to start by reading one piece at a time.

Well, after reading the first prose, I immediately went straight to the next one, then the next, and then the one after that. Her writing pulled me in and captivated my attention. I ended up sitting and reading over half the book without realizing it.

Needless to say, I more than enjoyed what I was reading. Few things had recently caught and held my wandering mind as well as this book has. Jessica's unique writing style is both refreshing and creatively inspiring. Her use of well-placed adjectives and rhythmic phrases painted beautiful images in my mind's eye; her written words I saw as clear and realistic as if I was looking at a museum painting.

Beyond the beautiful imagery painted by Jessica's words, something even deeper tugged at me. I can sum it up with one word: genuine.

The expressions, feelings, thoughts and ideas that are contained in her work all feel real and genuine. I've read many works, including my own, that felt forced and fabricated, written for the mere sake of just trying to create good literature. When done this way, the writing has a shallow feel with an aura of fakeness that's easily detected by the most layman of readers. That is not what I experienced in the slightest when I read *Crimson Sunshine*.

What I read were poems and proses built on foundations of real thoughts, genuine experiences, and honest expressions that pulled at my heartstrings. They awakened lost feelings of pleasant memories and nostalgia which moved me in many ways.

One of the hardest things to do as a writer is to transfer thoughts and feelings to words without having your writing become clichéd or what we call cheesy. Because Jessica's writing is so genuine and she has no fear using a bold textual style, her writing comes out as solid poetic and rhythmic prose that reach out and invite your mind and soul to go places that are both real and intriguing.

What I liked most about *Crimson Sunshine* was the storytelling woven within each prose. Some of the story aspects were obvious and others, which I loved, were less obvious. By reading between the lines, one can find masterful writing buried just below the surface. This book is filled with little golden nuggets that are worth a king's treasure when found.

Crimson Sunshine has an enjoyable depth that invited me to go back and reread. Each time I did, I found something new—the hallmark quality of a great piece of literature.

What I disliked about *Crimson Sunshine* was that it ended. I wanted to read more from Jessica's proverbial writing pen. My hope is that she continues to write books that I'll undoubtedly have the pleasure of losing myself in.

Surely everyone will enjoy this book as much as I have. My only warning is to make sure you have ample time reserved when you pick it up, because it will sweep you away in such a way that you will not desire or even have the thought of putting it down.

BRIAN R. HALL, Author
The Legendary Kingdoms of Attera
The Mountain Night Owl Tales

Poetry & Prose

2

3

FIREFLIES

I wish that I could contain you; grasping the special moments as the fireflies of our youth.

I could light my way brighter without stumbling in the dark—having unsure footing and racing heart.

If I could contain the beauty in every smile and embrace I would be immortal knowing death could never capture our soul.

If I could steal away every accumulated second we stood sure arm and arm together I would hold hope that there would be more—

More moments of fireflies.

More moments of us.

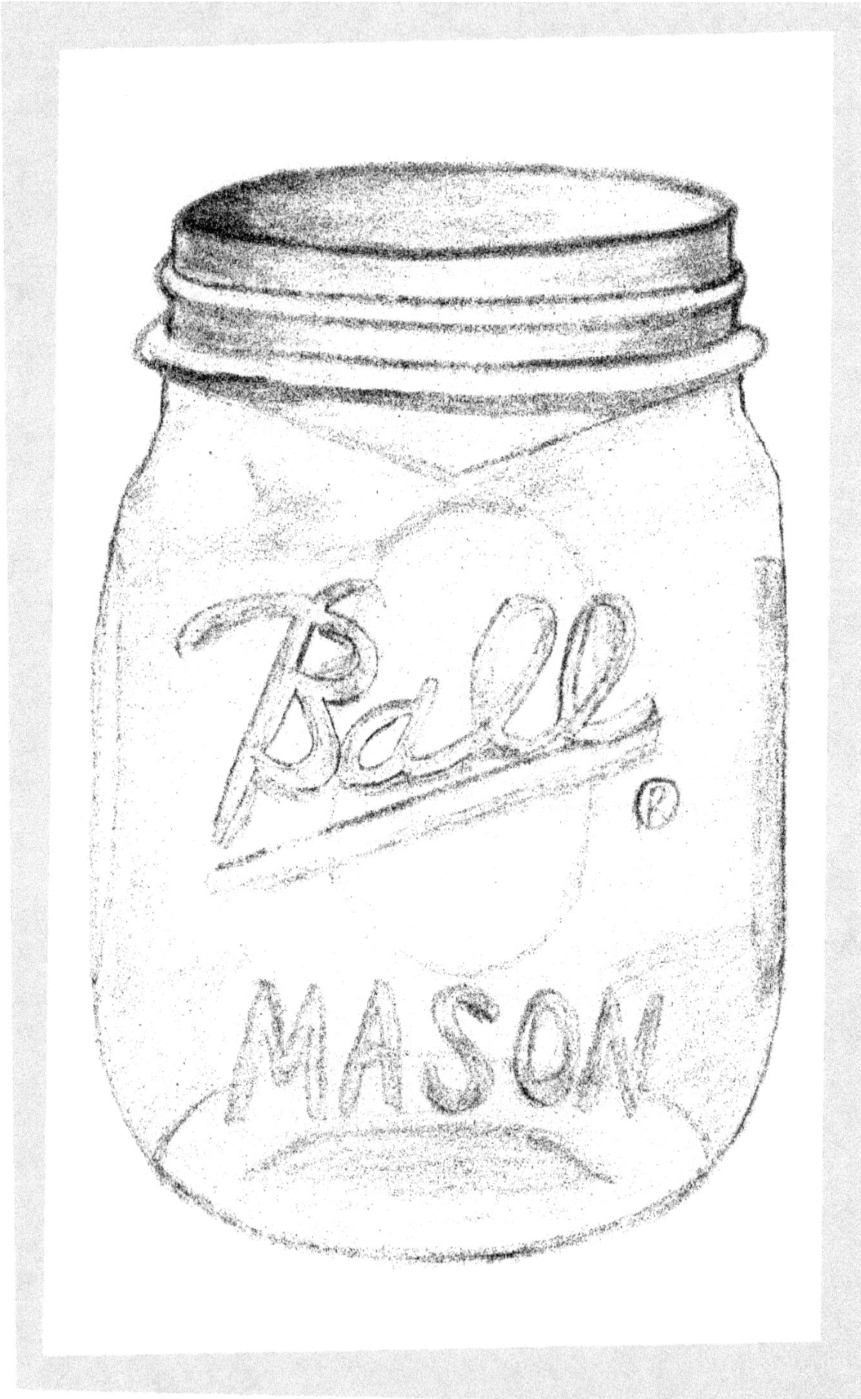

Ball
MASON

5

A PAST TIME

The dust brings youth and the crack of the bat; a reminder that this boy will refuse to stay a cherub no matter how fiercely I demand it.

His height is my death; edging me evermore toward the cliff face. I rejoice in my demise as he runs the bases, makes acquaintances, and catches grounders.

My spirit breathes in the precious mud and grass stains on his uniform, the smell of the new leather, and those blue eyes that sparkle while learning something new.

What a glorious distraction from my imminent old age; these hands more weathered than the glove he breaks in.

I watch in the sun—it is rising for him, and setting for me.

THE BICYCLING FISHERMAN

The marsh stains your denim overalls as the earth marries your cigar. You till the potatoes as your auger and poles wait patiently in the car.

Those gentle eyes and cheery smile—you married your love in 40.

Never straying from that one room floor except to the cold of the Aleutians in—World War II

What was that story—frozen toes and the solider buddies you cooked for. You proclaimed that hell had frozen over!

Your presence made me steady; your shoulders took the strain. I could be me again in the shadow of your protection. An oak—you shaded me well from monsters; some so real and some—nightmares.

To have you back again cleaning catfish in the beaming sun as guts were thrown about like decoration—my heart would burst.

You would curse as they horned you. But you taught them a lesson or two—with your frying pan.

A man of catfish and mushrooms; you in the kitchen with your copper bracelet gleaming. You whistling as it tempered your aching bones.

The yellow cabin roses fragrant in the summer heat as Grandmother peers from the washline.

A LETTER TO LEE

You never could handle goodbyes. The emotions left you uneasy—
never able to face the granite of your friend.

You did not bend that way—a pine Indian. Tennessee and Crockett
taught you that.

Men don't break in the wake of things, but you broke as her
vermilion hair did to chemo.

Your heart broke in two—at the aorta. My candles still hot with wax.

Our secret is—I had seen your tears before shed for me—in
frustration at your hesitance. A regret you confessed after
a few beers to loosen the cracks.

God—now to have you back in your Carhartt coat and leather boots.
You were my anchor—to him.

We anchored each other.

You with your tall tales and me with black hair and dark skin—just
like him.

You promised him and though you would deny it—you kept your word.

You always stood strong in the background of my story. A strong calloused hand to cling to.

Tell him now about our adventures together and stand proud in his presence—you shielded me as he would.

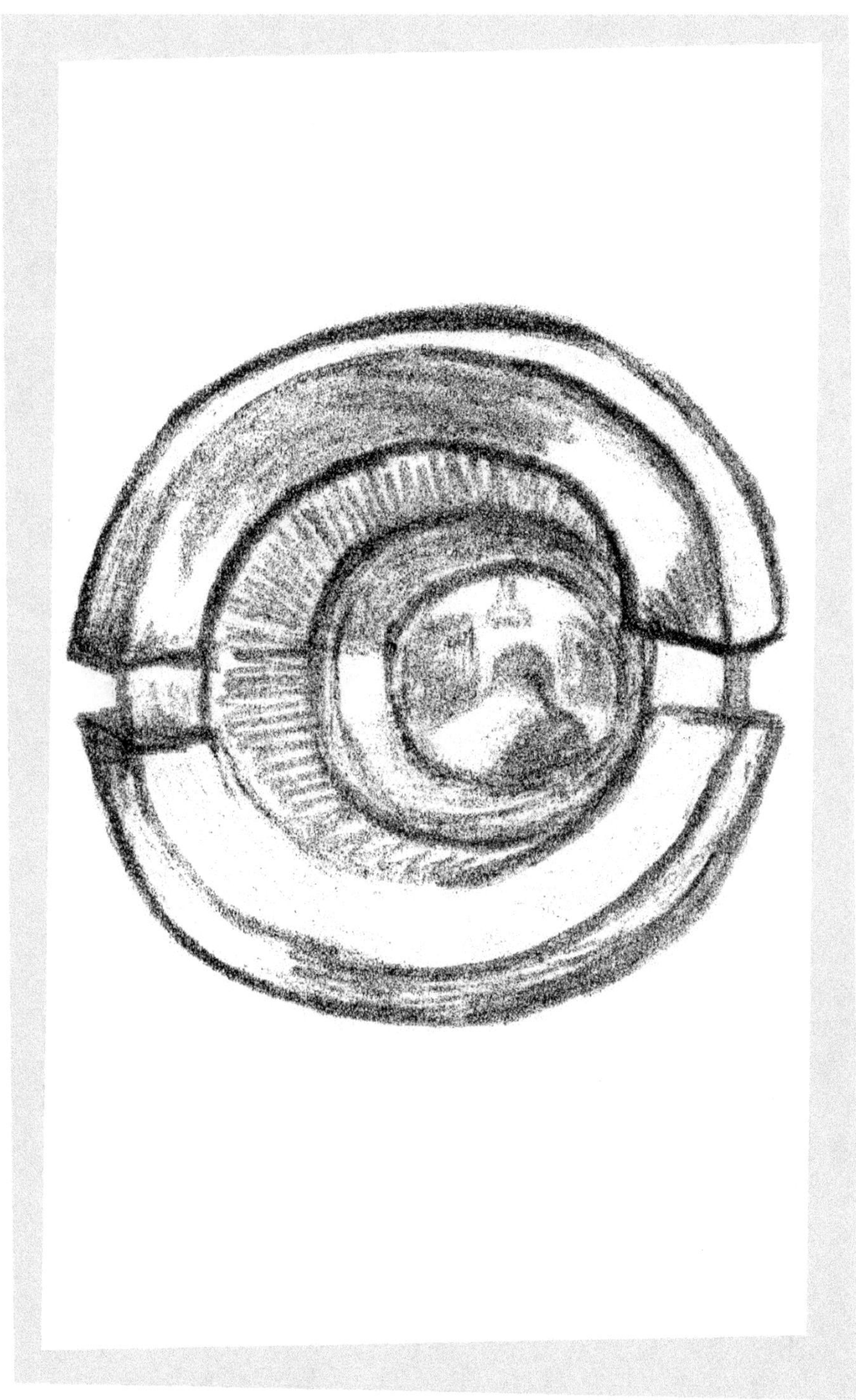

Thoughts & reflections

GOODNIGHT MOTHER

I always despised these concrete walls with no remnants of home—the home you invited me to.

The floors were slant and the doors ajar—a drafty mess.

Nevertheless, when filled with the love you filled it with, the worn carpet became an Egyptian rug.

Not like here with the beige walls—cold and hard like your IV pole.

You open your eyes and look at me, not able to converse but begging—

To go back to your small, dank rooms with worn doors. You begged for home.

I beg for it, too, now. My frame is worn, as yours was. The pain and age settling in as an old friend overstaying their welcome.

It throbs, but not as certain as my memory.

You motion for a drink of water, but you haven't enjoyed one for days—as the haze of life is escaping you.

You are leaving us too, in the quiet of the coal dust and the tiny worn down kitchen and old stove. The place that time ignored for hours as the flour swirled around us and magic was made.

But today there is no magician; just cold, hard pain—a cold summer rain ruining our quaint picnic. I am done with death, and one day it will finish with me.

How do I cling to that you taught me? How did you pretend so well? My regrets lay before me remembering that day on that rotted porch.

"Call me Mom," you said slyly, but I shied away uncomfortable; scurrying as if a field mouse. I redden to the memory.

My struggle to hold too tightly caused you to slip away before I could say "Mom," like you pleaded me to. You needed it for me, not you.

You were scared for my pain. I was scared for yours. Each begging God to tear it from the other. Pain is living. Now I live with yours and mine. This time with no slanted floors and I ache for those rooms.

This room does not warm like that coal camp house. Those rooms warmed with love, laughter, important matters found with God, hope, and books. No cold could penetrate. Death and pain stood at bay. You held them to their places.

The power you wielded I feel you did not understand. Our world in your hand turned to dust.

There is no returning, and I dream.

13

STRAWBERRY DREAMS

Our dream is walking and our love toddling—

Pouring her strawberry milk in a glass.

She sleepwalks—midnight stalks, but then lays down with her ringlet curls to rest.

A face of yours yet eyes of mine—

Strength all her own.

She lies there still angelic in the night.

Our heaven, her soul, and a strawberry mustache.

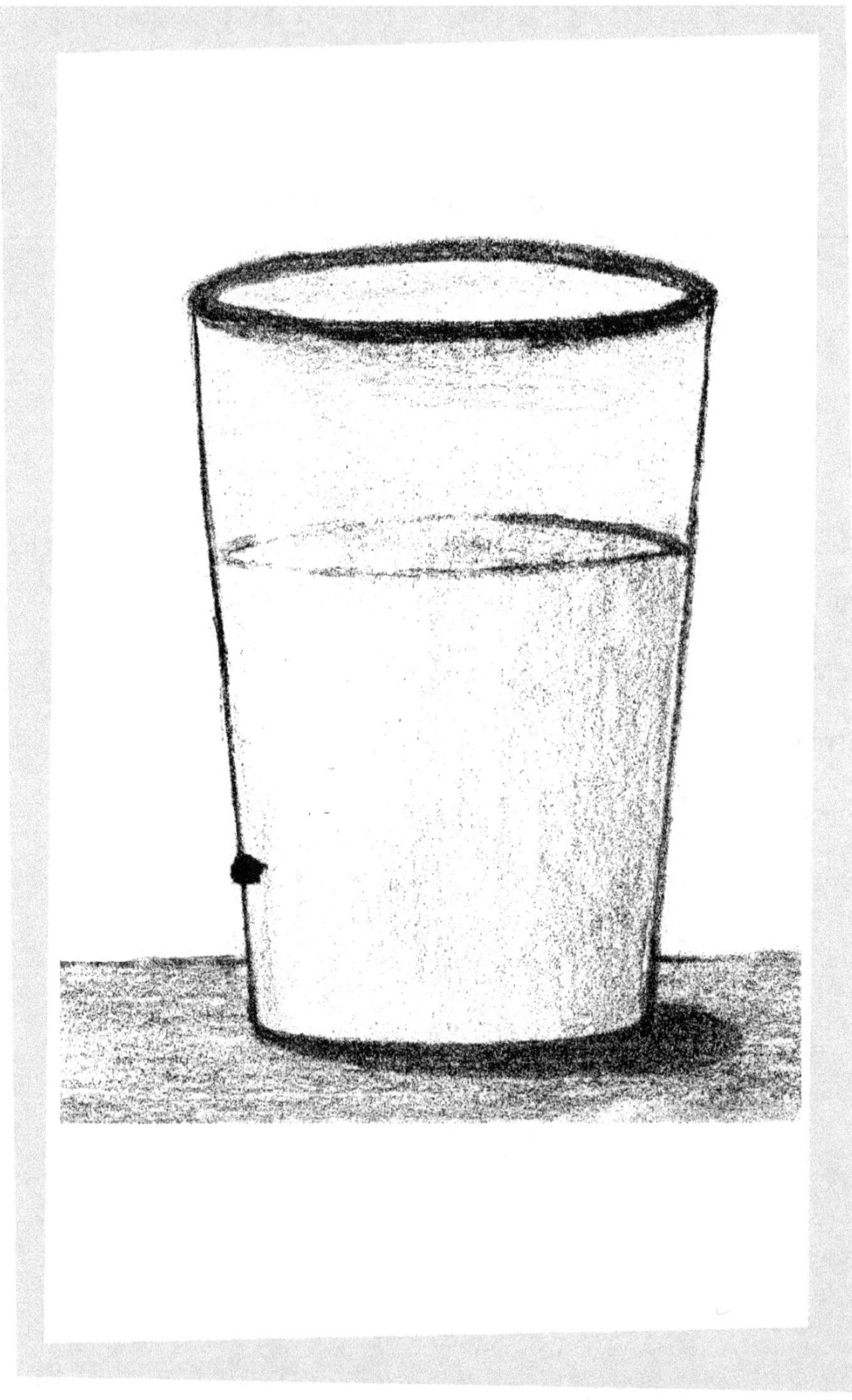

BEAVER CREEK

Southern summer comes to mind as wild honeysuckles fragrant the breeze. I recall a preacher singing baptismal hymns as he washes away the earthly sin—in Beaver Creek.

The water of dirt, coal, and clay turns sins pure as they go in—and come out new. The preacher, too. This is his second act today. His first was lovely, dark, and deep 40 feet below the hill he is preaching on.

Sunday comes and he is clean with just dark hints to where he has been—in his eyes and below his cufflinks.

His voice graces with sadness; subtle suffering detectable, unforgettable and his eyebrows wearily furrow—it makes him believable somehow.

He goes on his tirade to save while outside the coal gons limp by on hot tracks. The screeching steel driving these precious resources someplace else.

In the little white steeple his congregation cling to hope and the gospel. In a time where coal is going—gone in most places like an archaic accordion.

Preacher, sing of Galilee and let it echo through the pine with your melancholy strain. I see the tracks before me, preacher. I see the train. I fail to see the intended destination.

Lay me back in the water of coal, preacher; save my soul and make it whole again. Can you find the rest of it wherever it is you reach from to draw devotion—as you preach to the forsaken?

And trudge down again where no God has been beyond the streaks of black in the air so frail. The darkness of sin fails in comparison to that.

A place where time slips by, faster still, if this hill caves in—as we creatures do with sin.

Preacher, sing of Galilee and save the souls within.

DADDY

Your presence is announced like clockwork. The heavy thud of your lungs heaving as you climb the hill toward the gaped brown door.

The cough is so demanding and always on time as you arrive home.

How could you tell the hour so many feet below coal; down the shafts and beyond the elevator and veins of black?

There is no standing but crawling on bent knee or laying if need be on your back for 12 hours—

More now with this stranger's mouth to feed.

Your hacking is a telltale sign its morning. You climb the stairs to turn off my light. It was something we shared. Daily you would settle the fear a monster had started.

Praise God for your bleeding heart and blackened hands. The 30 years in coal did that. Forever stained like the bathtub she readied for you.

If I dare risk it, I could wander to a frame in time when she packed your sandwiches—antique Christmas heirlooms, so precious, but she knew what coal meant.

Men failed to come home from coal. Every night she anticipated it. I was too young to comprehend and she dared to hint at it.

She would fold the foil so gently, tugging the edges—pristine in the silver wrapping. She packed it in that coal-encrusted box.

But no dirt—just stained. She dared not wash it night after night—year after worrying year.

Pure love.

Pure sacrifice.

I learned those from you.

What position you had gotten yourself into but not as sure as Vietnam.

A pain you declare is off limits.

You escaped them both but not the wounds.

The deep begging your lungs are giving reveal exactly where you have been.

Coal saved us all and fed us too—in that tiny coal camp house. There were rows and rows of them standing still but ever so slanted and worn from time and the love within.

There were children in every room relying on your uniformed back of soot.

The weight it must have been, pressing, as if the air in the mine— thick and foreboding.

You never revealed it—not once.

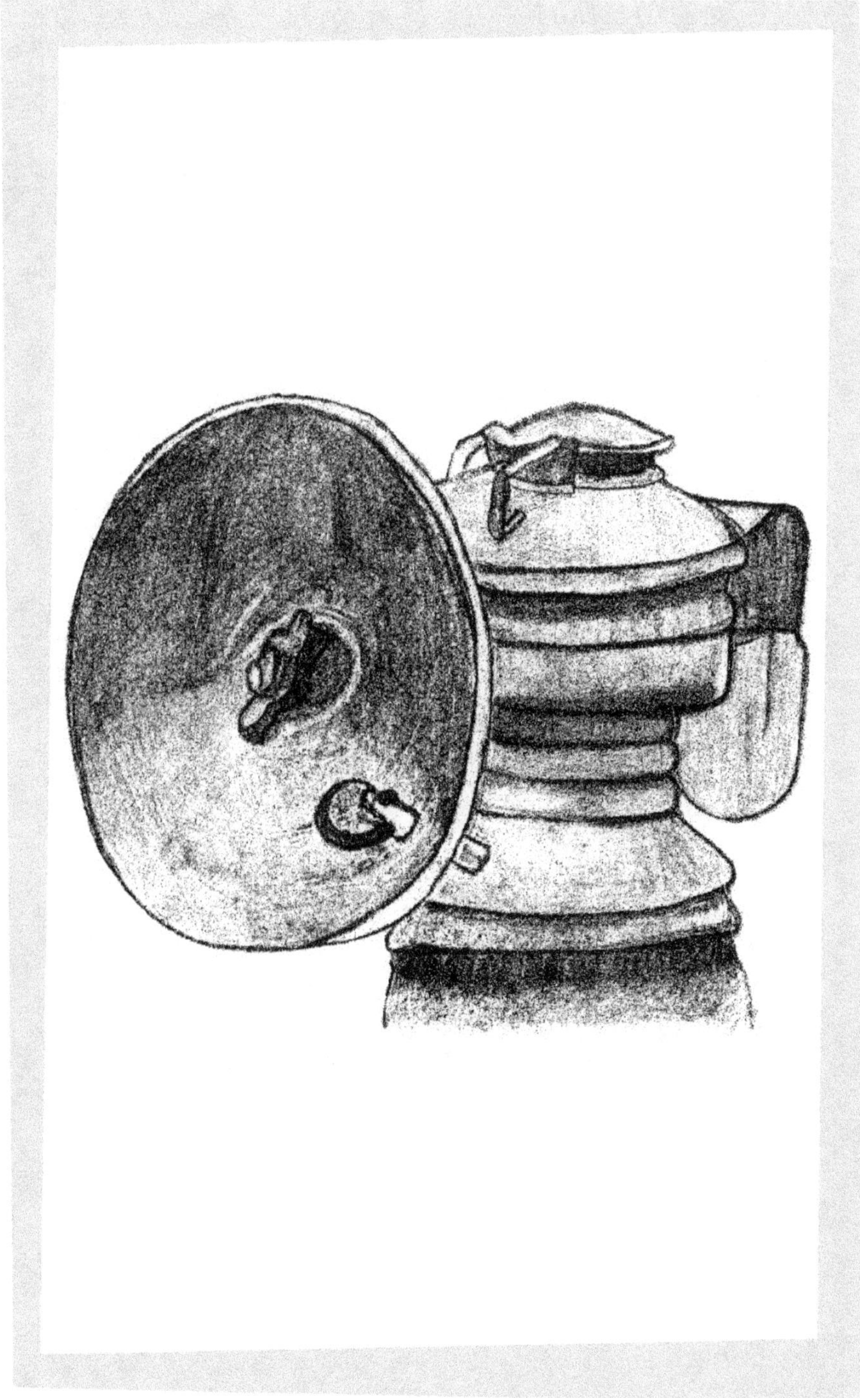

Thoughts & reflections

BIRCHIE

I see her now in my childhood mind; the four dank rooms she shuffled through—oxygen tank and cracked hands—the Lucky Strikes had done their work.

She had an odd way about her as she sat on her little couch; a coffee table near filled with ashtrays, crochet and quilt patterns.

She rocked slightly as if rocking her infant; maybe a habit she couldn't cast away. She had rocked thirteen babies since she herself was thirteen. A mother's way of holding on a little longer to the preciousness of being needed.

Her children were grown and a few had slipped away, but on Sunday her house was filled with their memories. Murmurings of their own children, their work in the mines or simply laughter to pass the molasses that was Appalachian time.

As they filed in she would scutter about the kitchen creating her masterpiece from pinto beans, lard, and flour. No one was allowed to cook but her—everyone washed their dish to show respect of their full bellies and quieted hearts.

For someone with meager means she fed us all—Jesus breaking bread. Instead hers was cornbread and blackberry dumplings.

On summer nights as a thunderstorm graced the sky, Birchie and I would swing on her front porch where laughter would turn to conversation and lessons on life.

We would retire; falling asleep to Rockford Files and her muffled snoring.

Birchie, she was not boring; a .22 under her pillow and a daily billow of smoke about her living room ceiling.

Her cough ever present as she painted her fingernails red, crocheting blankets and stitching quilts for the holidays ahead.

She was a constant for me though the rooms changed a bit from the four rooms to a hospital bed. We continued our nightly routine there too, though we watched Johnny Carson instead.

At night I would sleep in the orange chair next to her bed with the dread of leaving. One day soon we wouldn't swing again watching the rain, but I knew to relieve her from the strain meant I would be broken.

It broke too; my heart so big for her. With her last request, her nails were painted pink to match her jogging suit.

23

AMERICAN MUSCLE

We must let go the hands of giants becoming newly giant ourselves.

Our legs quivering beneath the reluctant title thrust upon us and the weight of the sparking eyes from below.

What are we but the dust of our fathers; the dirt from the earth they bring off their hands and jeans.

Tilling gardens of beans or working in oil under their favorite machines—

Jeeps and Blazers.

We are the dust of their dreams—their sands of time slipping between our fingers.

The remnants of their lasting souls trailing above.

We must let go the hands of giants reaching down for the young arms with our own.

Our dust beaming from below us as we push toward that which is our star; that place we settle in the maar of the galaxy completing this familial map evermore.

An ever encompassing geography; ebbing and flowing with dreams, dust and debris of love, triumphs and failures too—

Charted by giants for me and you to carry; finding our place beside them way too soon.

25

IN SITU

The smoke rises leaving love in embers. The gray cloud plumes snuffing out each of them.

The black billow sails us to the land of stone heads with names and dates to and fro never accounting for the wake from its trail.

Whenever smoke enters love will not prevail and age shall not.

The yellow stains remove years, remove time and silence laughter.

It is after the loveliness. It concaves hope into a mess on the floor as we watch the coroner at the door time and time again.

When smoke thrives love dies. The ultimate serial killer. One and then the other in sick procession—ripping the seams from this Rockwell tapestry.

We lose vibrancy within the blackness. Our anchors become weightless and float into the blue.

The smoke beacons as love turns its weathering bones towards the other room and no one pleads to enter.

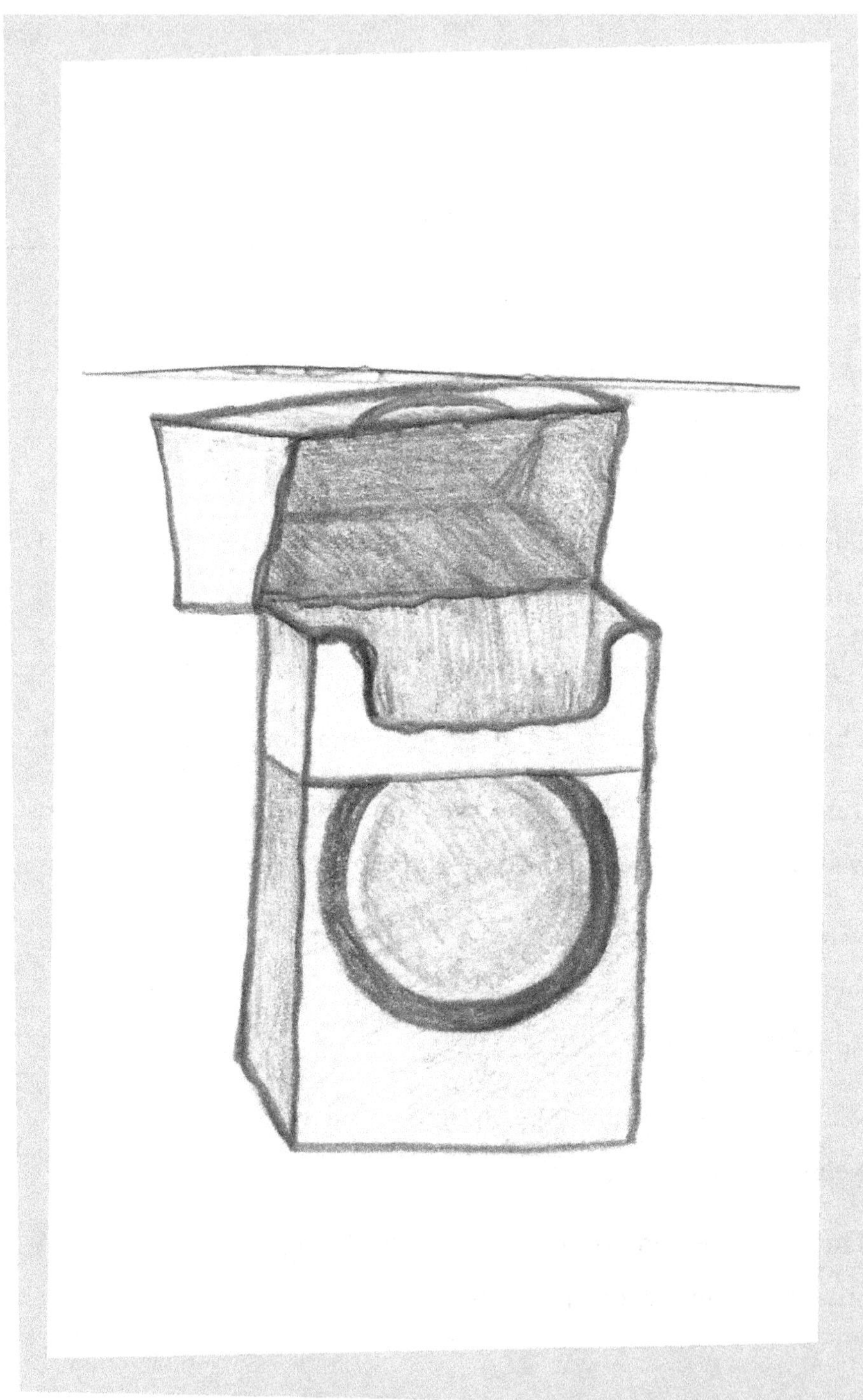

JIMMY

I had a dream and you were there—that golden hair and smiling eyes. That sideways look of yours that is so rare; you flashed it at me as if to say—no big deal, I am here.

I hugged your neck in that gentle way; the way you felt after a fresh shave. The skin smooth and the hint of Knize Ten.

Maybe it was you; maybe it was me conjuring up a wish so big. A wish to have you take me away to that place you went that day on that stretch of California road—

Your speed too free, like your soul.

Godspeed lost control.

But here you are debonair and next to me. The gel still wet in your hair—sitting in the theatre seat as we watch Fred Astaire—

Dancing.

You look at me and I feel the tone in your eyes. Your voice matching when you say—hey, it will be okay. But you cannot lie, not even you.

Jimmy, even you are not fast enough for my pain—nor can you absorb it like you wish to.

You stop—taking in the movie praying I would refuse to stay and wake from sleep.

PIKEVILLE NIGHTS

It was a place neither of us should have graced; a dirty bar for the hardened and jaded. You with friends and I with him, but there we were just the same.

The band played that southern twang with steel guitars—the singer rough and intoxicated. His days long passed and chained to his stage.

Your face could be noticed in every crowd, at least by me; you see, you and I are familiar. Time was spent side by side wood and rims—together.

But here we are; I am linked in his arm as you approach. I swallow hard as forever marched since our last conversation.

You hesitate; your blue eyes meet mine. You smile and nervously look up at him—high too—he towered over you but that, my friend, did not sway your question.

Can I dance with her, you muttered—just one dance you begged. He glanced down at me knowing it was needed.

The anticipation was stagnant. He walked away looking back as you took my hand—the band playing a slow one as if on cue.

You gazed at me, unhinging, as you always do. You pulled me close—
The dance floor swaying.

You are drunk on bourbon and me on your embrace—a chase I had
given up many years ago, our friendship and closeness a shadow.

Your eyes so piercing and smile deceiving as you tried to convince
me you were straight—your breath spoke otherwise.

You are living fast. I am trying to steady what life I have left. We
both had grown together, troubled in homes of constant turmoil.

I was finding sanctuary but you were digging in and this grin before
me now has grown as old as this song.

You glare over at him—are you marrying him, you ask? I see a hazy
vision—tears or perhaps inebriation.

I glimpse away and then back again as your pull is closing in;
believing it can will me to utter—no.

Yes, I say for certain; and yes, I said again—glancing over at the
anchor that is becoming my salvation.

You clutch your hand at my back; your grip is tighter still. This song
is groaning older and the room begins to spin.

You stare at me with knowing that you have only a minute to spare
before your moment is lost and the slippers turn to dust.

I love you—you mutter; breathless but with resolve as you know it
will not solve the loneliness of your heart.

Damn this song and my chest is tight with pain—shame for what you are becoming and the sadness as I let go.

I sense these final moments and whisper—I love you, too—you slow our swaying steps.

The crooner belts his last note to this ghastly, dusty song. You feel your meter expire and you lead me from the floor.

Your hand is cold and shaking but you walk me strong and true; whisking me over to him as you say—I give her back to you.

I catch your view as you turn to walk away. You glance back as if to say—I am sorry I have failed you so.

That was long ago and now no more words can be spoken as again you have forsaken me and left me to this world.

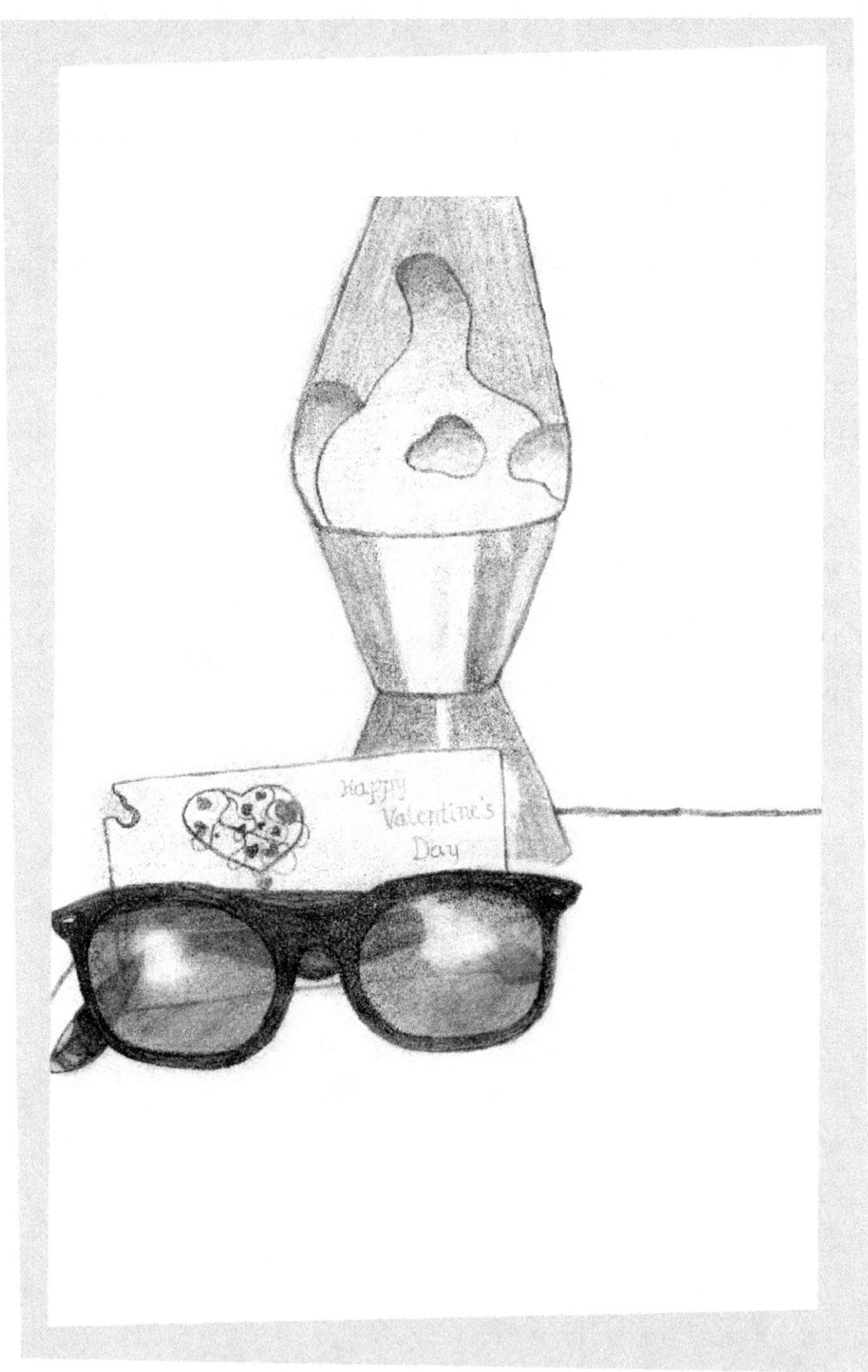
Happy
Valentine's
Day

33

MOREHEAD

I long for those moments. The leaves dance as we walk—hand in hand planning our little universe.

The horizon screams of autumn hue and the air bites my cheeks leaving rouge of red.

I scan the sky for stars; you scan my expression—staring at me as if you had roped the moon.

The before becomes blank; the after entwined. That was twenty autumns ago. Twenty years of orange, burnt sienna and fire. Twenty years of you.

THE GLOAMING

Beyond the green and everlasting haze; beyond the concrete and life's maze lies this path of uncertainty. It calls to me.

This world has shown me all that it will afford and I close the door to its salesman. I feel an urgency; hearing the call from the fields— hearing my dad's voice calling me home.

A voice of crystalline acceptance; withdrawing the never-ending ache that has a permanence in this frame. My form wilts and sways no longer withstanding the blows from the storm.

The hurricane rages with no ease, no reprieve and no mercy.

I call mercy.

I call sanctuary.

I call to my Daddy and he calls me home.

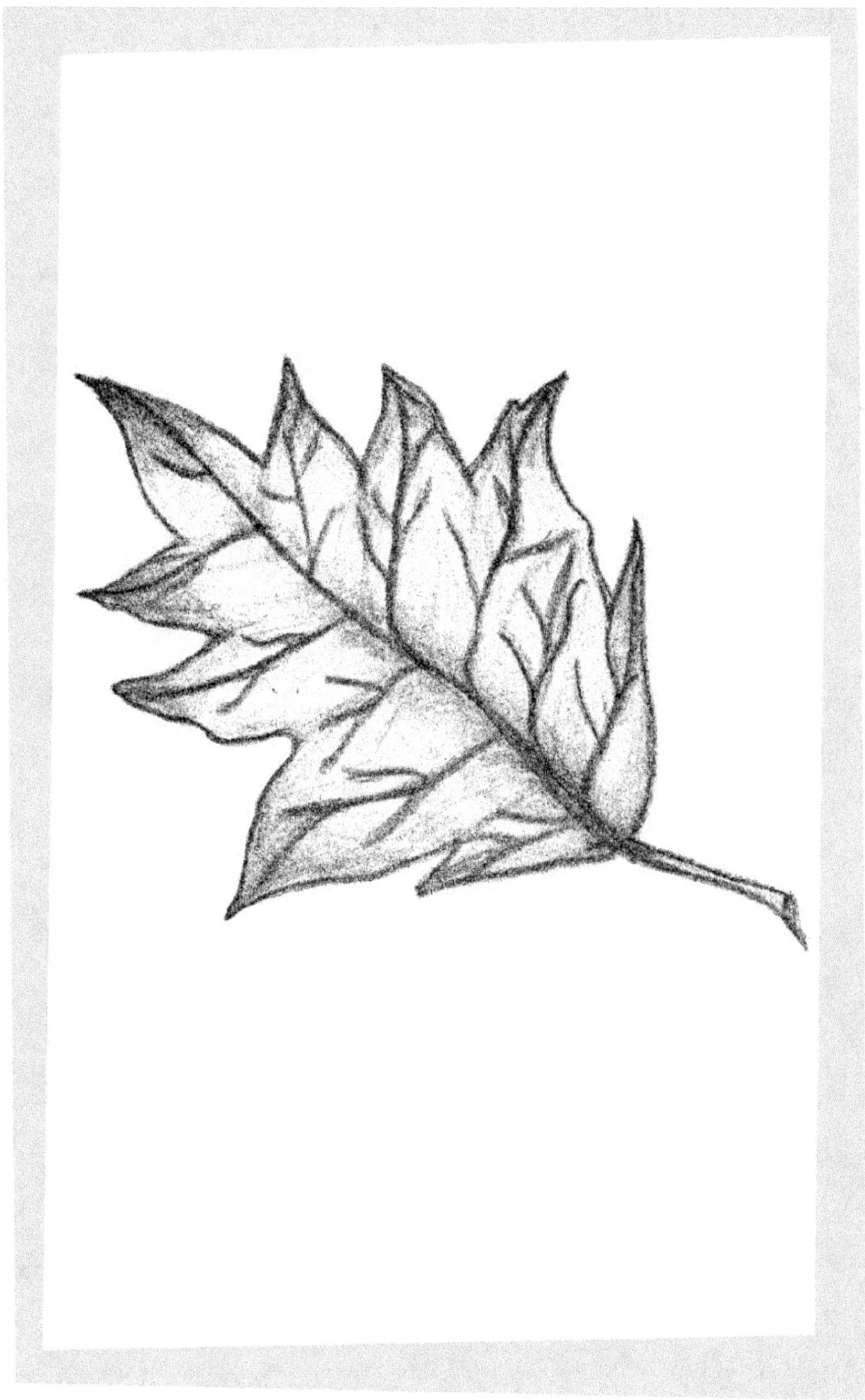

Thoughts & reflections

THE RISEN

I Will Rise this glorious morning with your body near me so warm. We will spend the day together; a calm before the storm.

I Will Rise after a sleepless night of a baby's deafening tears just to wake again tomorrow knowing I have to rise this way for years.

I Will Rise when the flag is tattered and the tags are bloody and worn. I will rise again when they call my name to send me away once more.

I Will Rise from this cardboard home with my toes frozen like clay. I will stretch my aching back to search dumpsters for the day.

I Will Rise to assess the bruises and to find the courage to pack my bag. I will convince myself it's now or never; or an ending with a coroner's tag.

I Will Rise to make that appointment with hope that the news is good. I will rise again tomorrow praying the treatment took as it should.

I Will Rise with my voice shaking to stop the violence within these walls. I may not stop the pain, but at least I rose at all.

I Will Rise for you my darling, my love, my light; though I did not want to rise at all—barely making it through the night.

I Will Rise even when you tell me it is not within me to rise. I will stand strong on unsure legs never affording you to see me cry.

I Will Rise when my body cannot rise and my Jesus holds my face. My voice—my soul trembling as I envelop his unwavering grace.

OMEGA

A quiet shudder, the sudden stir—the air so stiff with Christmas allure.

My words fail me as the feeling is so strange the night before sweet Jesus came.

It is a quiet excitement yet melancholy noise. My heart rises up but stops for a pause.

It seems I started living yet died just the same the eve of the night that Jesus came.

I lose my diction. My hands start to fail. The air is so thick with a crystalline smell.

His spirit flows through me yet dances around, but I cannot see it though the sense is profound.

I lose all emotion as I whisper his name. I feel my knees buckle on the eve of His day.

How can others not sense the ghost of this man? How can they not marvel at his imminent plan?

I stand on the bridge with my eyes strained to the sky. I scream out my words but I cannot cry.

It must be the feeling so many have felt when they knew he was coming and they prayed as they knelt.

This feeling escapes me and yet still lays its claim every eve of the night that our dear Jesus came.

41

TEMPUS FUGIT

In the smallest things that become profound; when time beckons to hasten and the winds die down.

A butterfly, an ocean breeze, the honeysuckle—the cottonwood floating in the trees as if an impostor.

A clasp of another, a glance—a dance. A single minute stretches its charms.

A miracle we can never comprehend.

A whisper from God—Himself.

A single second gains the hours' hand.

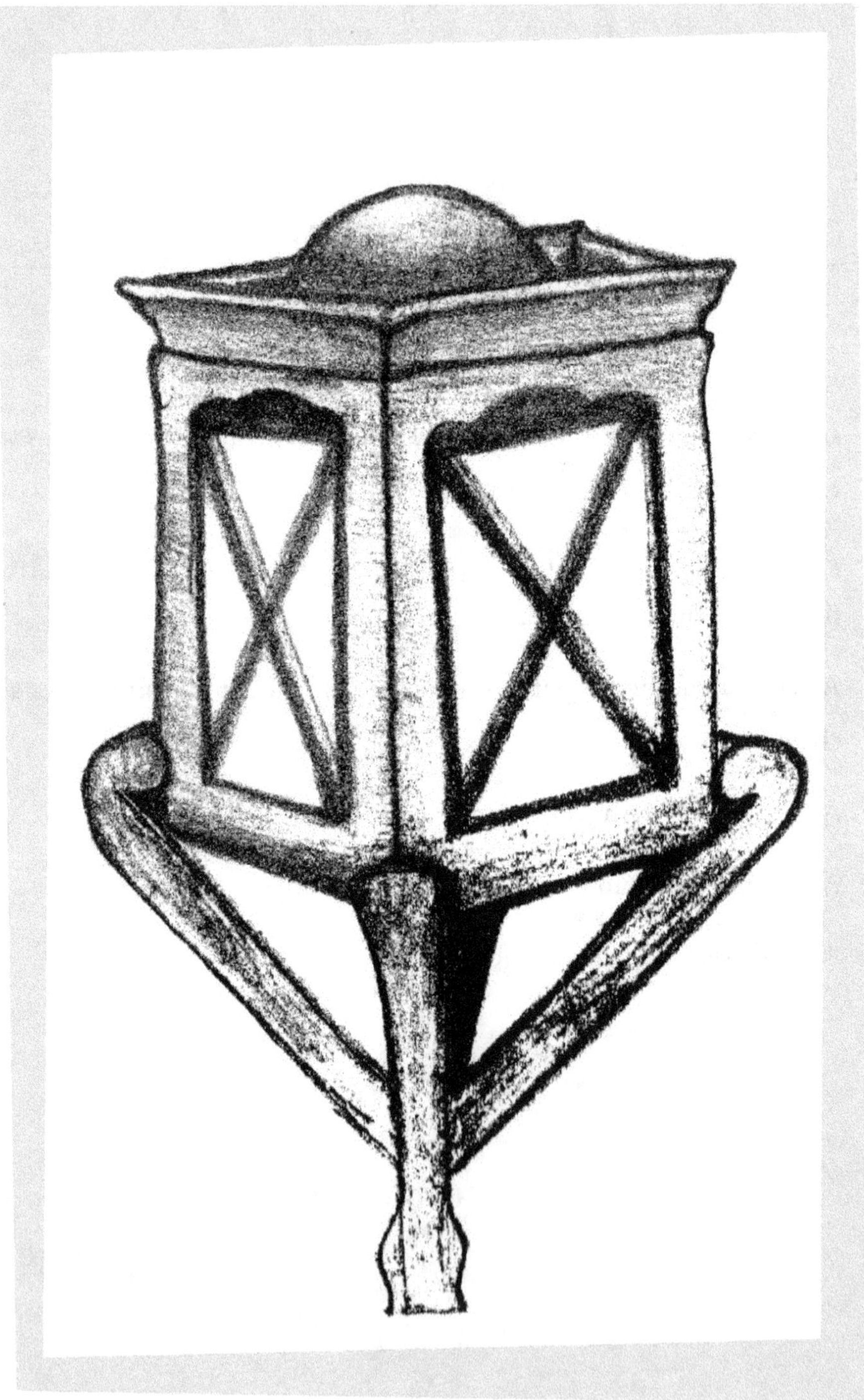

ARLINGTON

Our glory drapes its tattered slain for a country unforgiving.

The parade—a façade of apple pie and tickertape softening the blood and agenda.

Red, white and blue death becomes the normal truth for our youth.

We deliver up our boys; angelic, strong and new. We are delivered broken men; some so broken only a body bag can contain their pieces.

No mother's arms or word of prayer can repair their brain or savagery of what they sustained or bore witness.

The aftermath is relentless agitation, aggression, confusion and those bore the lucky straw.

The rest lay out in crisp uniform and bloody faces—succumbing alone in mud, stone and sand—

Trying to protect a foreign land who forsake them in the name of a country who dismiss their dog tags.

The only welcome home now is a black box and stiff flag. Our stars and stripes ride high with haggard breath—the sand stained red.

Sign them up boys—send them in. There seems to be a few more reserved spaces in Arlington where wives lay on graves crying for that which could have been.

Glory's price has rose with inflation and this war is aging with no reprieve.

Everyone loves a parade.

MONSTERS AMONG US

In the wake of things life shakes out the uncertainties to reveal the solid foundations to cling to. We prayed that was you.

You appeared a man on a white horse. But a showman for sure—a liar for certain.

In youth it was discovered in more ways than one how the devil is evil in a kind face, but your soul—you failed to tame.

The blackness was evident and it followed you as she did.

A thief for sure you lifted it all but me. I refused to go easily—I would not go at all.

Too stubborn like my father, I surmise.

A loose cannon that would shake your façade and I could shake it still—let's see what spills you.

The note is gone and my heritage, too—a huge price to pay—I pay quaintly. It is steep and mounting but my conscious is crystal and my soul is mine.

A monster indeed, you know what I am implying. There is no denying you served yourself a huge pot.

Your due is stomping hard across the floor of your front porch. It is ringing the bell and the chimes are brazen.

For a score as big as yours the note comes full and it makes the current interest rate laughable—insurmountable.

Your shell cannot begin to drip that which is due but He will wring it from you.

Every drop of fear you forced on someone else in the night.

The screams are heard beyond the chambers that hold your eternity. At least that is what I pray for—a prayer long overdue and I, too, risk my soul to wish it.

I am free—intact and whole.

But your ravaged and twisted soul—

The bill comes due.

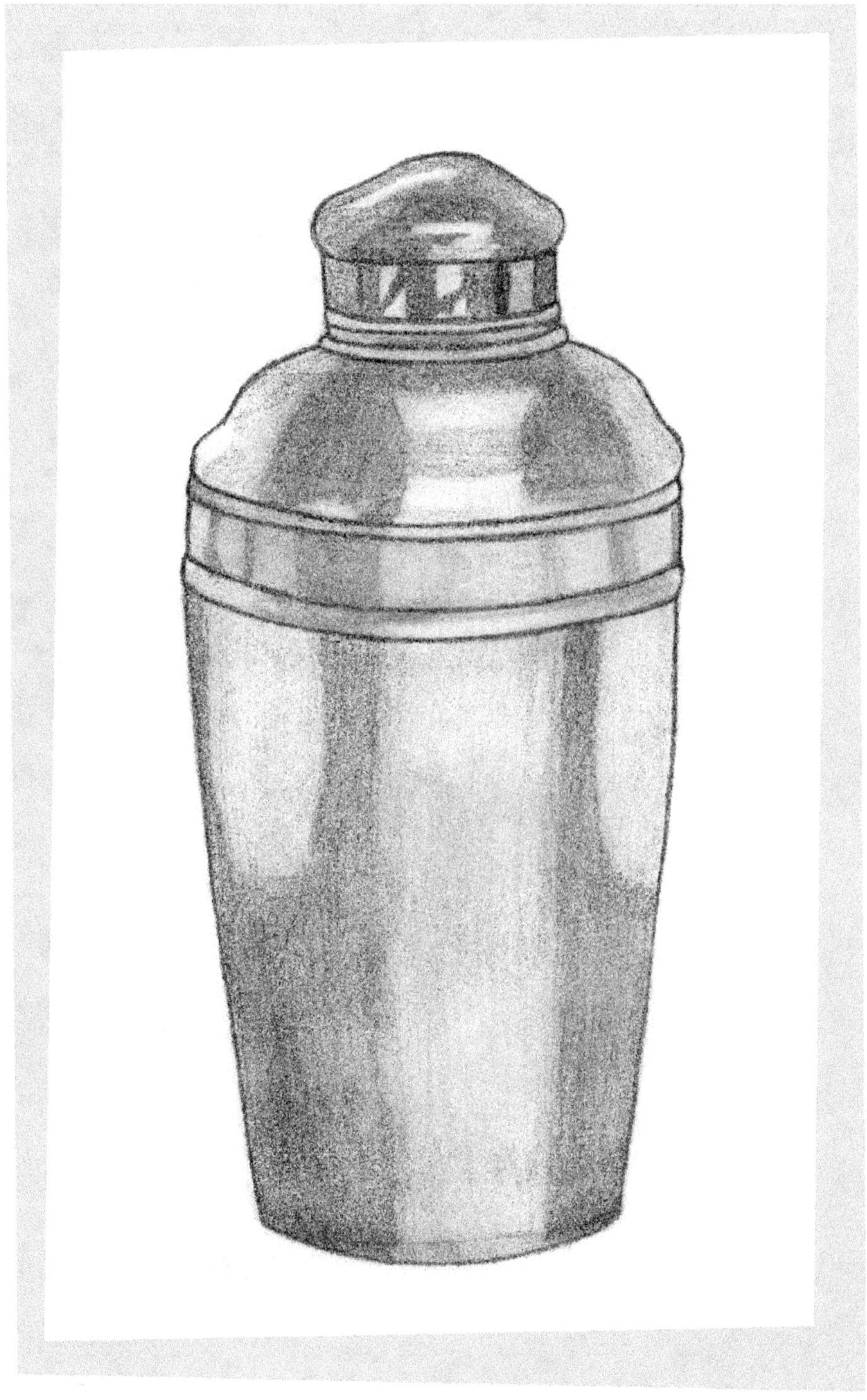

Thoughts & reflections

CHRONIC COMPANION

The teeth are seething, piercing my spine. The sinew breaks with recovery unacceptable.

Every tick is a snail's mucous pace—wakefulness be damned.

Hope slowly slaughtered with every eve of day. The sea's salt grinds every wound.

I blink.

I lose.

This merry-go-round is a whore. The excitement and the nausea all at once rise up as you give your all to claw a bleeding grasp. You stop sick and then ask for more.

Life is heroin. It leaves you numb, addicted, and strung out for another hue of that burning hue of morning simply to be disappointed by the gray of the next mundane pain of day.

The teeth are seething.

The sinew breaks.

KNIVES

The blade you yield is too dull for the purpose. On good days I pray you never reveal it. On those days when the sun strikes too hard, I wish I could sharpen it for you, ensuring it finds its place.

The blade is credulous and the waiting is hell. A damned hell—the ache cumbersome.

Shall I yield my own blade—finding the curtains. Alleviating these reciprocal blows.

End this—

Break me before I do.

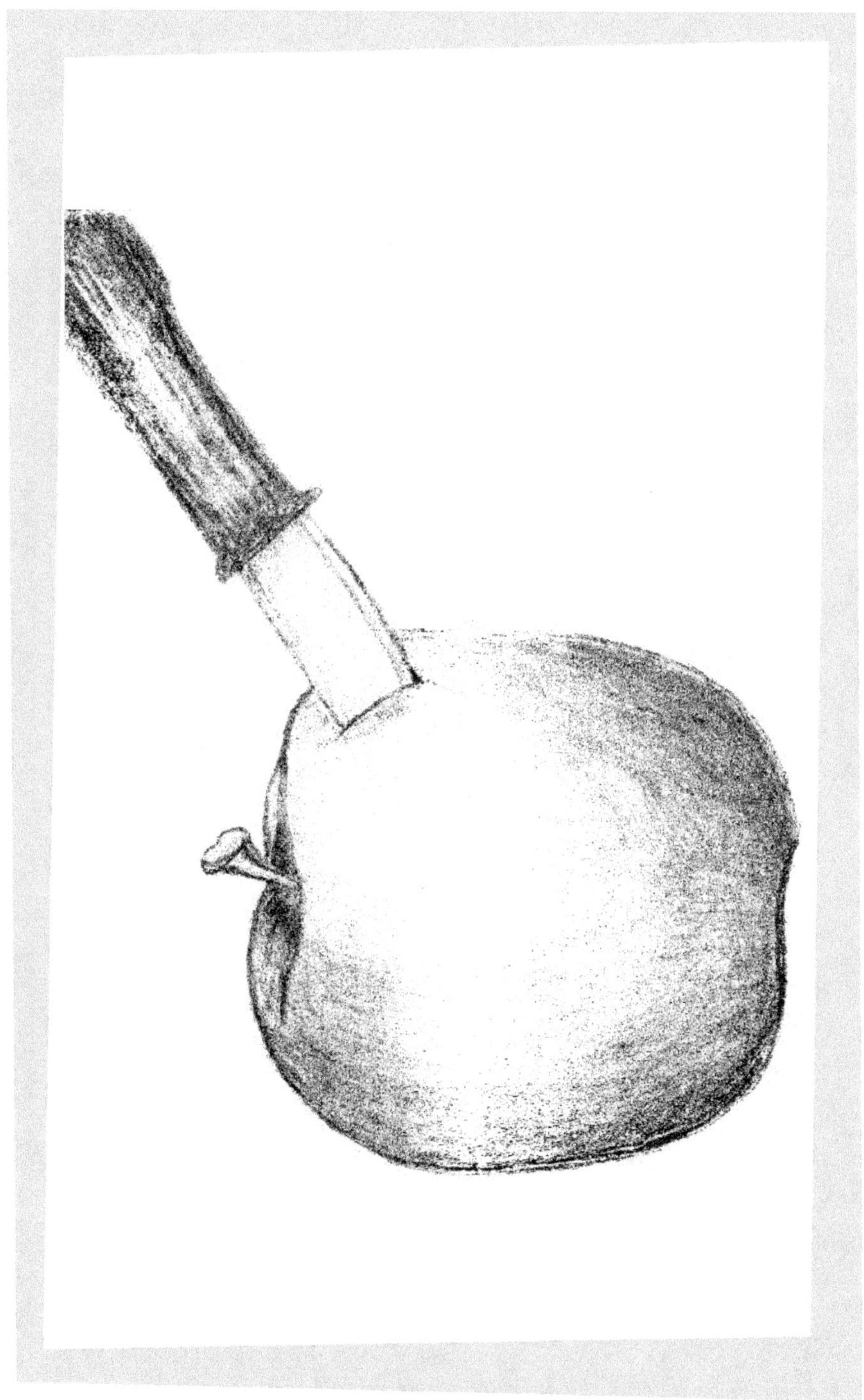

Thoughts & reflections

53

THE SQUALL

I sustain; blocking the silhouette of pain that forced the doubt and darkness into this façade.

Spending years trying to grin away the scars only to watch them deepen to the marrow.

The nerves are crazed—electric with no lucid thought contained.

No voucher for sanctuary.

This squall, a cold relentless downpour; there is no willow, no lean-to and no reprieve.

With simplicity and grace we survive day after searing day. The mirror never braves to show such a profile.

Only this image of dead paint, dead words, and no faint trace of innocence steering us clear of purpose and removing our vibrancy.

INDIGO BEACON

I dream in technicolor and live in shades of gray.

The fabric of essence slips between the crawlspace through the cracks created by my own insanity.

These days are mundane, coarse and the painting fades from exposure.

I lose composure. I scream into my pillow as the grayness invades my burgundy heart.

I beg for a morsel of change; a shred of amnesia. My tears burn of scorched tragedies.

Bodies of love that held me, championed me or never met me as their mother.

The covers grow heavy and the limbs flaccid.

Succumbing ever more into the deep hue.

A brazen blue humming in the wake. Never able to break the shoal. Busting the rudder to shards.

Infinitely steering in circles.

O 2

What breath I have is breath earned with yearning.

This breath is ragged and heaving.

I kidnap its O2—a last word of wisdom in a world now deaf.

Breath laboring and full of sand—stinging of fire ants.

It is my breath.

Breath molded—breath branded with nails.

My breath to spend on that which is worthy of expiration.

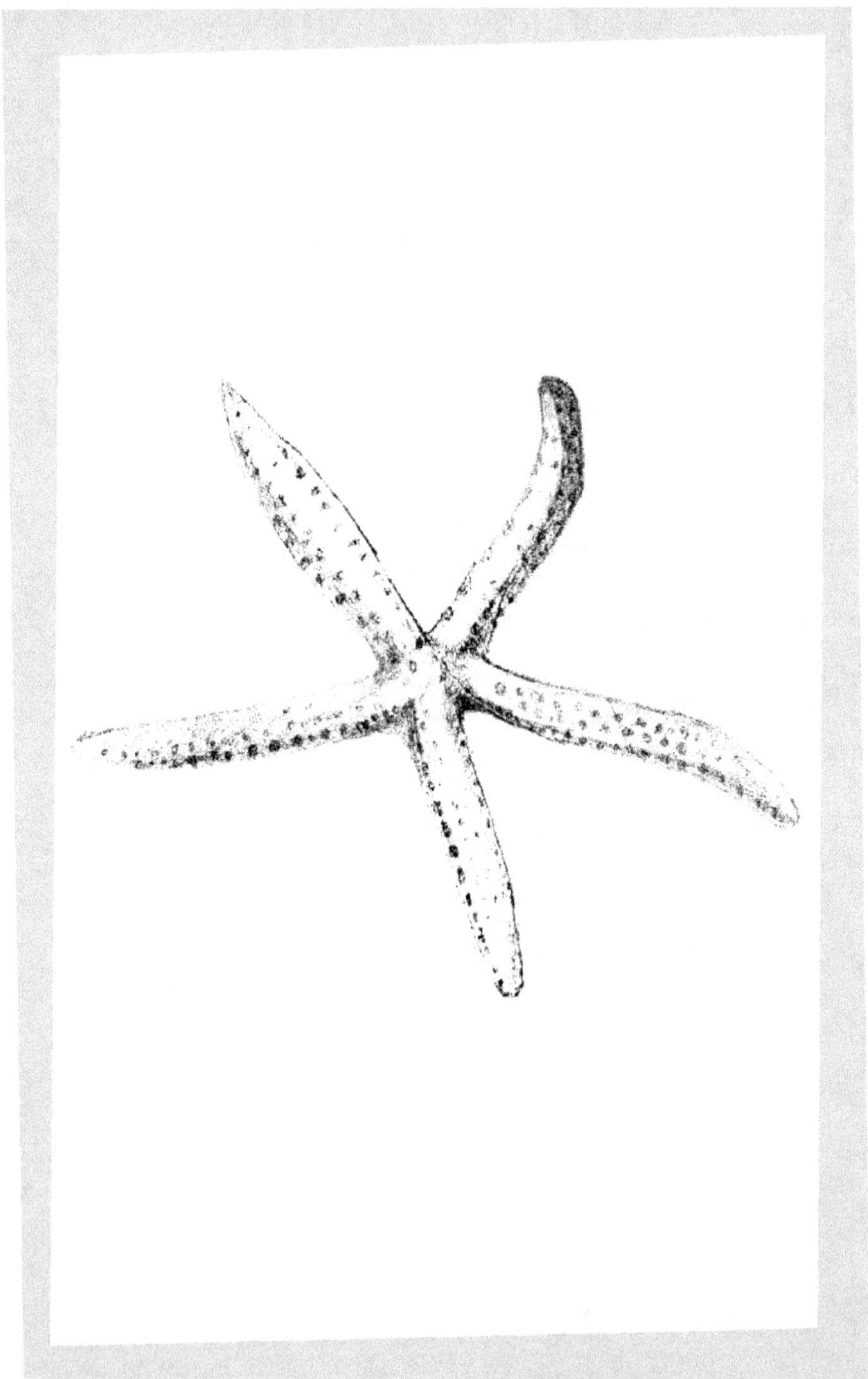

GARDEN GATE

In the garden the greenery blooms, reaching for Heaven as the sun shows. Forever hoping to reach their summit—growing slender and deeper in beauty.

I imagine flowers as the acrylics of God; touching up this world relieving its edge. The softening violet and blushed pale pink express hope on a canvas of concrete and crimson.

In the garden beyond glory's gate His own flowers give rise to home. The eclectic beauty of so many souls defining the edges of his streets of gold.

A garden welcoming of those who peer in awaiting his loving sanctuary.

Thoughts & reflections

VENUS

I stood and the moon stood with me. The lonely know their own. The losses have been so many and the road, my God, has been too long.

To look around at all this beauty yet dismiss it in the same glance is such a sin.

I do it often, and too often, I imagine, than God wishes for me to offend.

What lies beyond, I do not understand. What lies within denies me still. I cope with both the best I know, with coffee and Percocet.

The beginning was sunsets and pink dresses; the latter is old bras and chipped nails.

The between hits hard with a dirty punch and a boot to the throat.

The gray and black reside with flecks of metallic coat.

I squint my eyes to see her edges; small with hopeful eyes and taunt skin.

I cannot begin to pull that rug knowing she would fight her battles again.

I push her hard—breaking the skin as her legs fight against the marble floor.

In that door is the biggest monster—the largest black that shall encompass her even more.

GLASS AND ROSES

What's done is done. I ache as the panes crack in this glass house. The flowers wilt in the demise of the gloaming.

There is no glow in your gaze as you glance at me.

You refuse to dance with me, converse with me and no longer provide me counsel.

I am responsible.

Too broken for you to repair and the water is seeping in—cold and damp.

The figure of you, valiant; cannot stop this dam from raging.

My body burns—it aches of longing.

Time abandoned us.

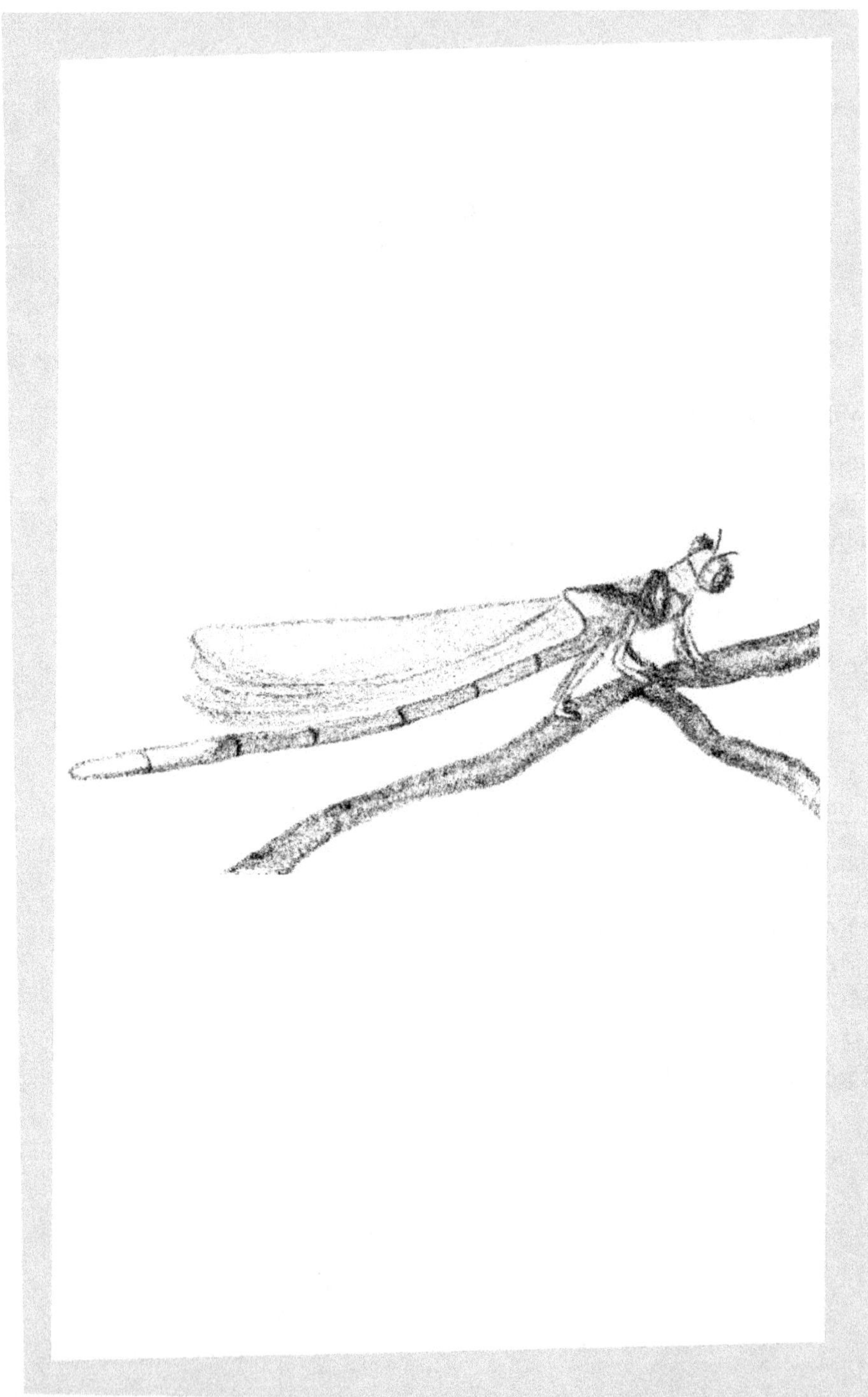

THE TANGO

Death breathes within us rising as the sea—so sure.

Dancing its ominous tap dance—rhythmic.

Whispering delicate songs—amore.

Though the urge is never to court it. The romance—the sleep brings you in.

Willing us to know it—an effort to dance the dance within.

We can will it to turn rapping—loud tapping that shatter the teeth and annoy the spine.

In that instance—releasing death to find another only to court you another time.

We may simply choose to sway to the music—hypnotized by its sweet song.

Knowing against all knowing that your love is in it—giving in.

My love—it is so strong.

64

DANSEUSE

I stand quieted by the dancer's pirouette.

Her pale dress blankets the haze.

Effortlessly, she glides comforting embers of anger igniting this soul.

65

ICE CASTLES

I ponder ice skates and the frozen stream you lead me to before you lost that starry night and my life went gray.

The shining steel and tassels hang tapping against the leather in sway to the motion of our walk.

Together—this image of midday in the winter sun.

Your fated hand in mine.

I ponder ice skates.

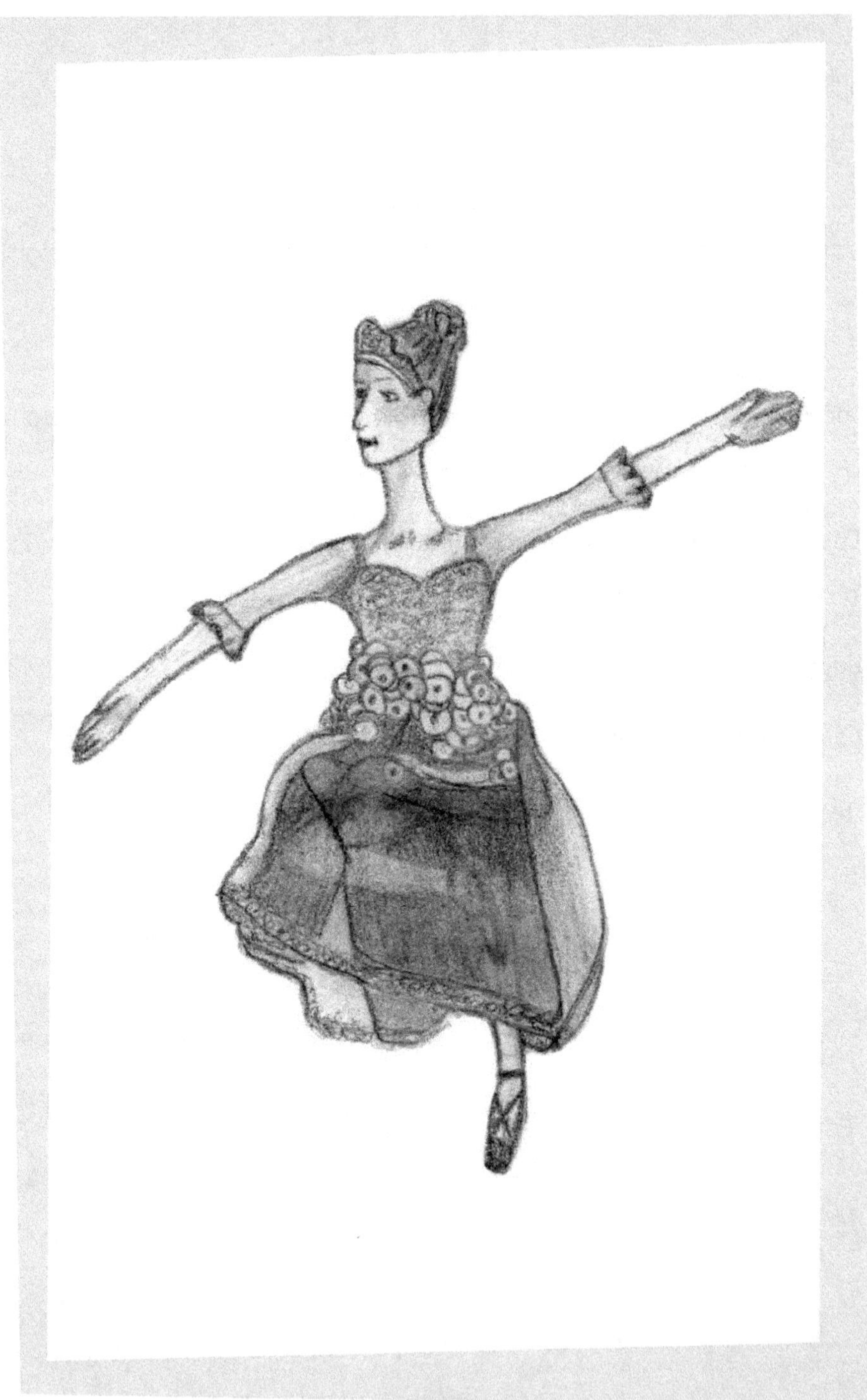

CAMELOT

Hush now, little dragon, so your strength can rise within.

Listen from your ashes—slither from your sin.

Steady your soul, little dragon—your wings are tattered and your tail frayed.

Others will put out the flames your anger and rage have made.

Your nostrils still are smoldering. Your village is all afraid.

Hide yourself little dragon—so much damage your pain has paid.

Curl up within your shelter—your scales healing from the blaze.
Await that one to rescue you from the scars your torch has scathed.

68

O Z

The rainbow ends.

The hues flake and crack as if it were an antique table that was loved too much.

The colors grow dim as the light becomes more defiant than it once was.

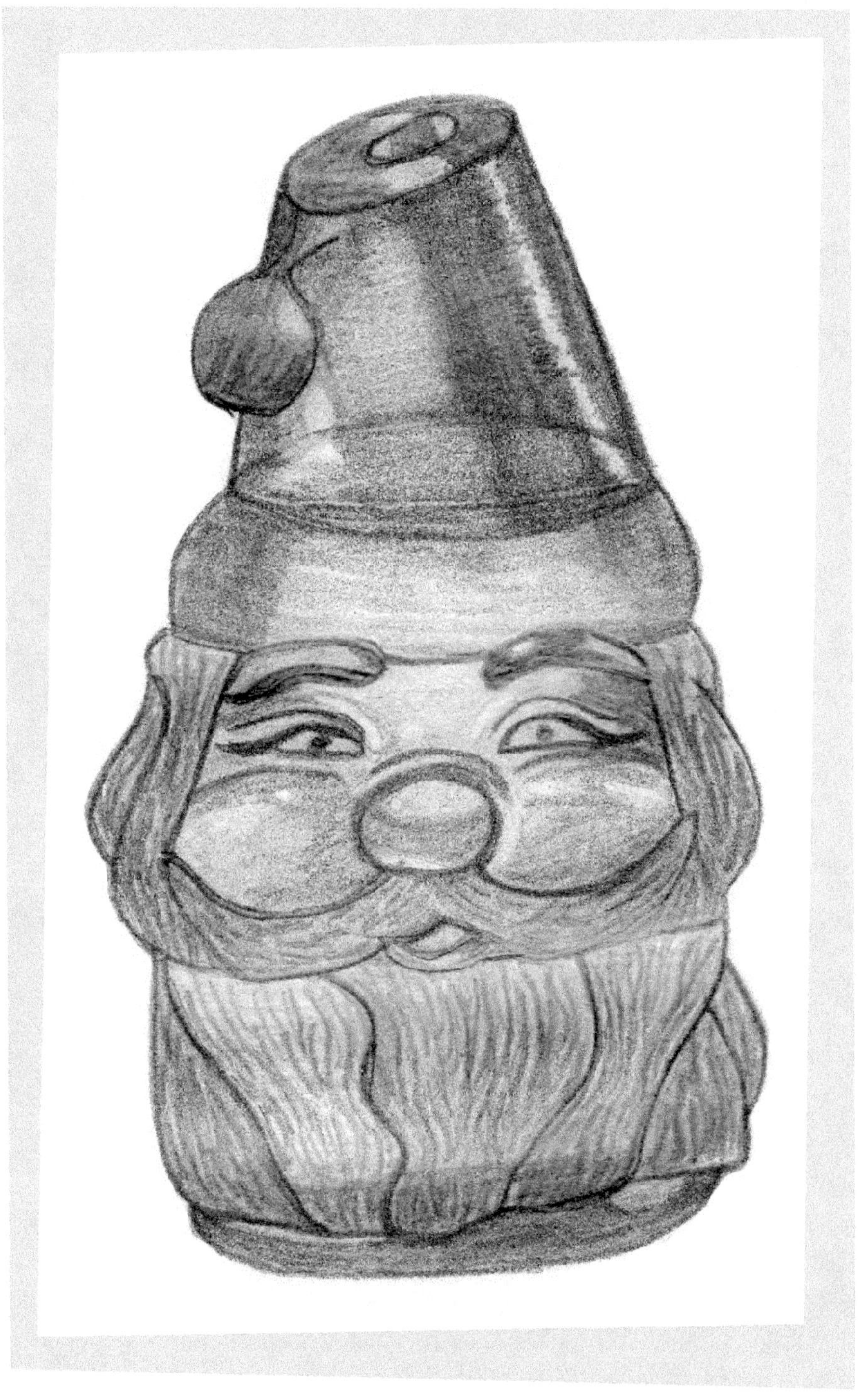

Thoughts & reflections

71

THE CROW

Be still, my wounded bird

Discover me within your wing

Replenish my second chances

Shall I wound you once more—My Love

Thoughts & reflections

THE ONE

My eyes grow dim with death. This breath I draw is labored and these limbs grow drawn and numb.

Hold me, Mother, like the night beneath the stars as the strangers from afar traveled to see this promise—anew.

Rock me the way you used to; cradled within your arms. Your heart beats as mine did—a glorious, harmonious tune.

Goodnight, Mother

My wounds begin to scream and these thorns rake my sweating, swollen brow.

I can still hear them now; taunting at my name as my frame begins to buckle and my ribs begin to strain.

Don't cry, Mother

Please still and don't lay blame. Their ignorance clouds the name of the Savior to deliver them home.

Goodnight, Mother

The stillness settles in.....

My eyes fail me......

Rock me, Mother, as you used to.

Cradle me as I leave this world like the night you brought me in.

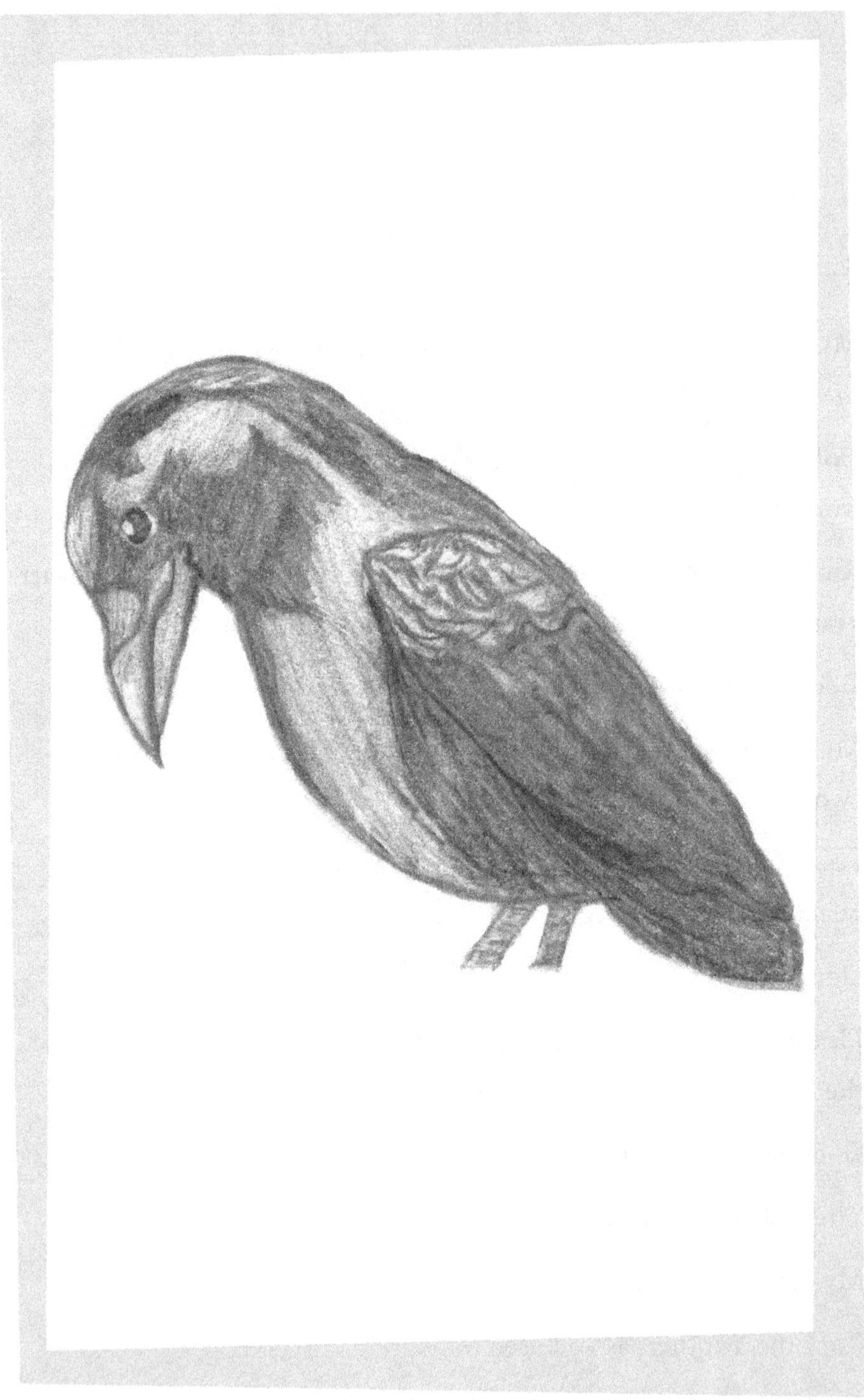

75

SILENT VISITOR

In curious amazement I found Heaven's splendor donned in white muffling the hum of the streetcars relieving the sharpness of fall.

Effortlessly it twists and sways in the disturbance of the concrete streets. Peculiarly perching—awaiting a ride on a red dress coat only to be scurried away by the gesture of a hand.

This silent visitor appeared to be dancing, a ballerina on her stage; forgetting those around her as she is lost within the orchestra.

There is nothing to compare to this silence. The most peace I have dared to witness. Only death I stretch to imagine could ever allow such distinction—

Blanketing this world with a frigid quilt.

76

SUMMER SNOW

The cottonwood hints of July snow as I walk gingerly row upon row of company kept.

They lay patiently in the wood and I ponder if they stood here as I do in quiet despair.

I will lay beneath the grass, wood, and sky awaiting a melancholy visitor; intimately being kissed by the cottonwood of July.

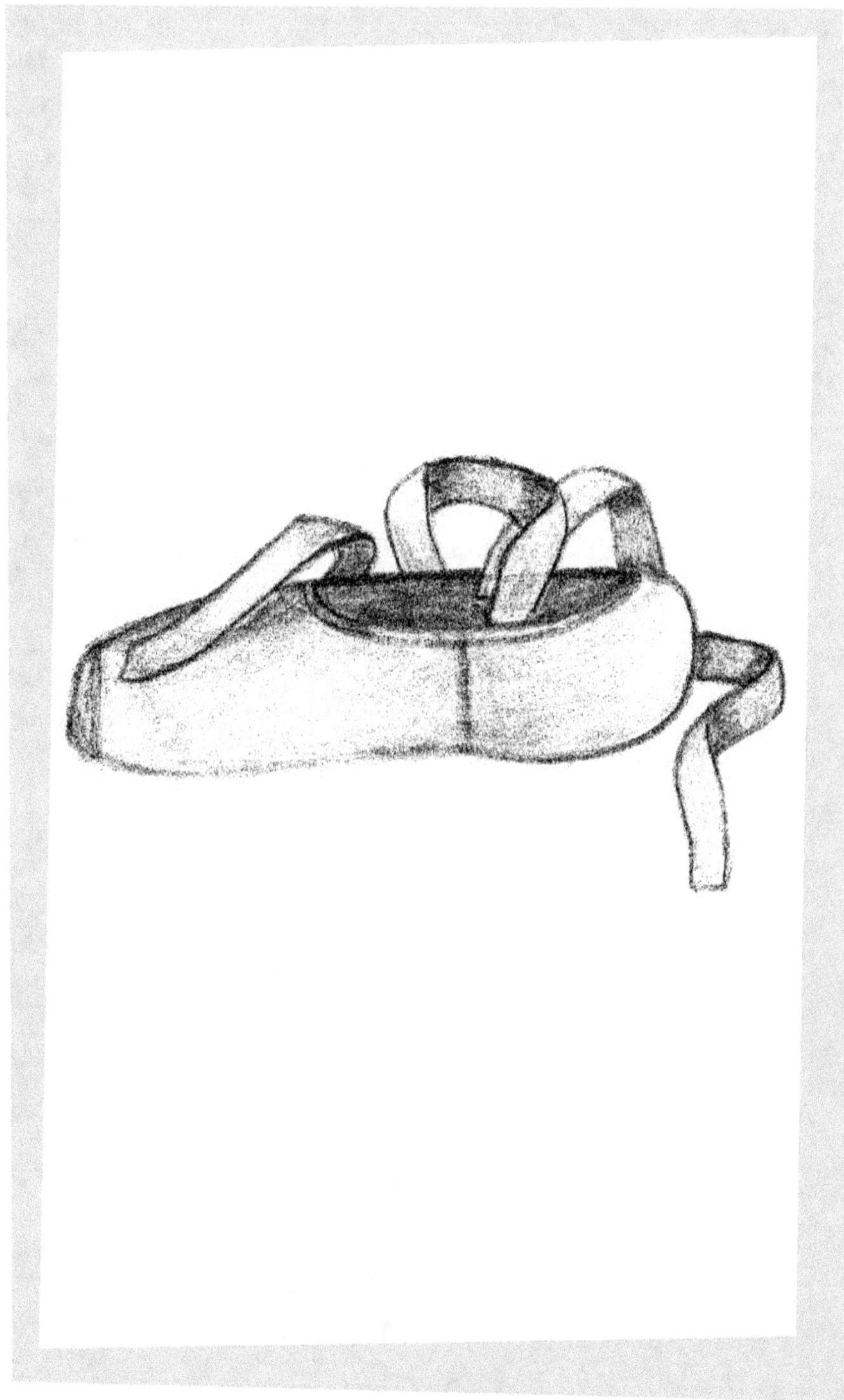

Thoughts & reflections

Thank you

Throughout life I've had so many individuals who became a safe haven for me; angels, if you will, who protected me, inspired me, educated me, encouraged me, and simply loved me, giving me wings to fly. Without the support of so many people, we are unable to grow, mature, and thrive to become the people we want and need to be.

At the top of my list is, as always, my husband Larry, who has been my best friend since we were children. Larry is truly an answer to a prayer made years ago, and he has saved me in every way a human can be saved. He has been my rock in every aspect of life since I was fourteen. I will never be able to express my gratitude to him, nor to God for sending such a loving and kind human being into my life.

I must also thank Lynda Cheldelin Fell for taking a chance on me and giving me the venue to get this book published. She has been amazing in this process and I appreciate all the collaboration and direction she has given me in my first book of poetry. What an amazing, inspiring and strong woman Lynda is, and I appreciate having her in my corner.

I would like to thank my daughter Laura Bentley who worked tirelessly day and night on the illustrations for this book. She is an amazing talent whose gift has elevated my words to a standard they do not deserve, and for that I am forever grateful. With that, Laura and I would like to thank The Ohio State University for the grant gifted to Laura for work on the illustrations as part of this project. The Ohio State University is an amazing university who inspire students to reach for the stars and stretch their horizons, as they have done for Laura. We are forever indebted for their generosity.

A thank-you must be paid to Mrs. Kelly Wells, Laura's former art teacher at Upper Scioto Valley High School, who has given Laura guidance with her illustrations, and collaborated on this project where needed. She is a very talented and dedicated teacher who pushed Laura to always give her best in her work. Even when Laura felt she had taken a project as far is it could go, Kelly showed Laura that there is always more an artist can give.

I would like to thank Brian Hall who agreed to write the foreword for my book and gave me advice about writing itself. Brian is an amazing writer with several books under his belt. I felt more knowledgeable and secure with him in my corner to bounce ideas off of. As a writer, you need talented individuals to help stretch your ability and push for what you're trying to obtain. Brian has done that, and in the process, opened my eyes to new possibilities.

Last, but certainly in no way least, I would like to thank all those who have given me wings—the Bentley family, grandparents, aunts, uncles, cousins, teachers, coworkers, friends, and my son Joe, who have all lifted me up in times of need. Honestly, every single life that has touched mine in a positive way has given me the power and strength to not only write these words, but also inspired me in living my life, striving to do better, and always giving me a sense of belonging.

I am forever grateful to so many, and you know who you are.

JESSICA WEYER BENTLEY

ABOUT

Jessica Weyer Bentley

Jessica Weyer Bentley is a poet, writer, volunteer and speaker who began writing poetry at a very young age. It has served as a therapeutic outlet, and she continues to hone her craft through life.

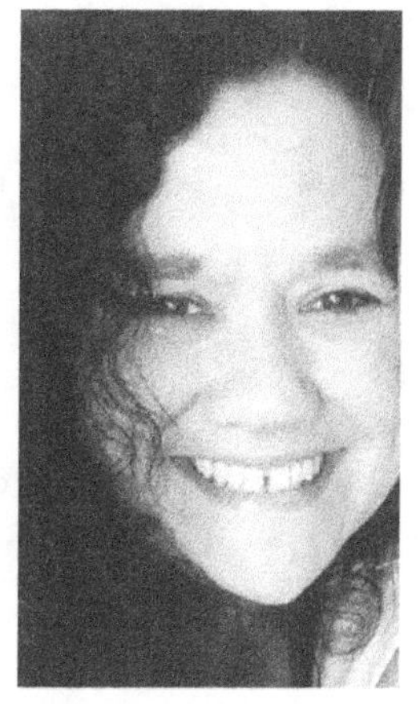

Jessica's work is published in *Grief Diaries: Poetry & Prose and More*, and *Grief Diaries: Hit by Drunk Driver*. She serves as a speaker and educator for Candace Lightner's foundation We Save Lives, and also supports law enforcement at sobriety checkpoints and other community events focused on impaired driving awareness.

Jessica spent most of her childhood and young adult years growing up in the foothills of eastern Kentucky, where she met her husband Larry of twenty-six years. They now reside in her native Hardin County, Ohio. She is the mother of two children, Laura and Joseph. For more information, email bentleyjessica@hotmail.com.

ABOUT

Laura Bentley

Laura Bentley has a bachelor's degree in Psychology with minors in French and Studio Art, and is currently studying to become a school psychologist at The Ohio State University.

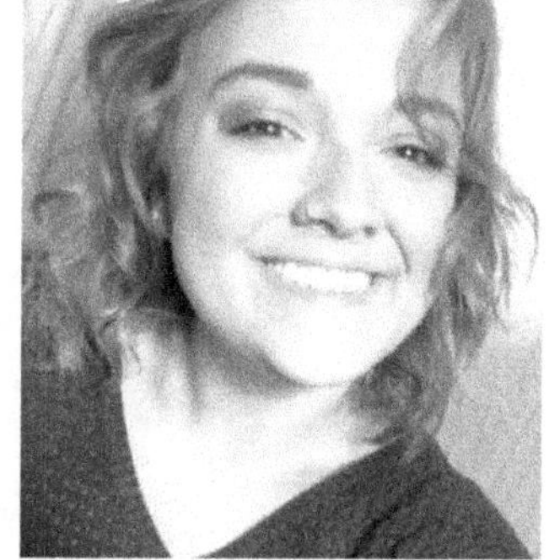

A piece of Laura's white charcoal artwork was featured in the Kewpee Art Invitational at ArtSpace/Lima in Lima, Ohio, in 2015. She won the Silver Key award in the Scholastic Art & Writing Awards in 2015, and her colored pencil artwork was featured in the Fort Wayne Museum of Art. Laura focuses on her studies and research in child development, and integrates artistic endeavors into her educational experience through her Studio Art minor. She continues to work with her preferred methods of drawing in various types of pencil while also expanding her horizons with printmaking and ink wash methods. Laura plans to further her studies in school psychology while continuing to practice drawing in different media.

Humanity's legacy of stories and storytelling
is the most precious we have.

DORIS LESSING

*

ALYBLUE MEDIA TITLES

Molly & Me
Barely Breathing
Faces of Resilience
Faith, Grief & Pass the Chocolate Pudding
A Child is Missing: A True Story
A Child is Missing: Searching for Justice
Heaven Talks to Children
Grammy Visits From Heaven
Grandpa Visits From Heaven
Color My Soul Whole
Grief Reiki
Real Life Diaries: Living with Mental Illness
Real Life Diaries: Living with Gastroparesis
Real Life Diaries: Living with Endometriosis
Real Life Diaries: Living with Rheumatic Disease
Real Life Diaries: Living with a Brain Injury
Real Life Diaries: Through the Eyes of DID
Real Life Diaries: Through the Eyes of an Eating Disorder
Real Life Diaries: Through the Eyes of a Funeral Director
Grief Diaries: Surviving Sudden Loss
Grief Diaries: Surviving Loss by Cancer
Grief Diaries: Surviving Loss of a Spouse
Grief Diaries: Surviving Loss of a Child
Grief Diaries: Surviving Loss of a Sibling
Grief Diaries: Surviving Loss of a Parent
Grief Diaries: Surviving Loss of an Infant
Grief Diaries: Surviving Loss of a Loved One
Grief Diaries: Surviving Loss by Suicide
Grief Diaries: Surviving Loss of Health
Grief Diaries: How to Help the Newly Bereaved
Grief Diaries: Surviving Loss by Impaired Driving
Grief Diaries: Surviving Loss by Homicide
Grief Diaries: Surviving Loss of a Pregnancy
Grief Diaries: Grieving for the Living
Grief Diaries: Shattered
Grief Diaries: Project Cold Case
Grief Diaries: Poetry & Prose and More
Grief Diaries: Through the Eyes of Men
Grief Diaries: Will We Survive?
Grief Diaries: Hit by Impaired Driver

PUBLISHED BY ALYBLUE MEDIA
Inside every human is a story worth sharing.
www.AlyBlueMedia.com

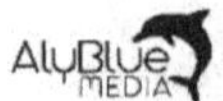